The Body
Brain

Veronica Ross

Chrysalis Children's Books

First published in the UK in 2004 by
Chrysalis Children's Books,
An imprint of Chrysalis Books Group PLC
The Chrysalis Building, Bramley Road, London W10 6SP

ISBN 1 84458 091 1

British Library Cataloguing in Publication Data
for this book is available from the British Library.

Editorial manager: Joyce Bentley
Editors: Rosalind Beckman, Joe Fullman
Illustrator: Chris Forsey
Designer: Wladek Szechter
Picture researcher: Jenny Barlow

Printed in China

10 9 8 7 6 5 4 3 2 1

Words in **bold** can be found in Words to remember on page 30.

Picture credits
Angela Hampton/Family Life Picture Library: FC (Inset) 4, 6, 11, 14, 16, 20, 23, 27.
Corbis : Maurizio Valdarnini FC, 9; Tim Kiusalaas FC (Inset), 26;.Tom Stewart FC (Inset), 15; CORBIS 1, 12; O'Brien Productions 5; Ed Bock 8, 25; Jennie Woodcock/Reflections Photolibrary 17, 21; Donna Day 19.

Digital Vision: FC (Inset) 22, 24.
Getty Images: 13.
Rex Features: Edward Garner 18.
Illustrations: Chris Forsey 7, 10, 28, 29, back cover (inset).

Contents

Look at me! 4

Where is my brain? 6

What does my brain do? 8

How does my brain work? 10

Thinking hard 12

Muscle control 14

Staying alive 16

The senses 18

Learning and memory 20

Feeling happy, feeling sad 22

Asleep and dreaming 24

Looking after your brain 26

Memory game 28

Words to remember 30

Index 32

Look at me!

I can ride a bike and read a book. I can talk and think and move. My **brain** allows me to do all these things. It **controls** everything I do.

Your brain gives you the ability to feel happy and to laugh at a funny story.

Your brain also
helps you to learn new skills,
like skipping.

Where is my brain?

Your brain takes up most of the space inside your head. It is a pinkish-grey colour and looks a like a large, wrinkly walnut.

You can't see your brain, but it controls controls everything you do, all the time.

If you were able to touch your brain, it would feel like soft butter.

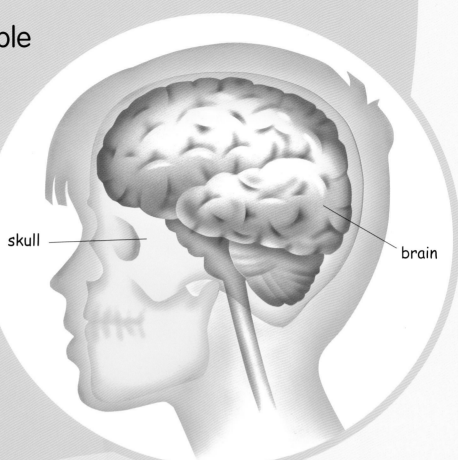

skull

brain

If you could look inside your head, you would see that your brain is wrinkled all over. A hard, bony case, called a **skull**, **protects** your brain.

An adult's brain weighs about 1.4 kilograms. The brain of a blue whale, the largest animal in the world, is much heavier. It weighs 6 kilograms.

What does my brain do?

Your brain is more powerful than even the fastest computer. It is the place where you think, remember and daydream.

A computer has a big **memory**, but it doesn't think and feel like you do.

It looks after your body and tells it how to work. Your brain makes you who you are.

Your brain lets you work out how to do difficult sums.

How does my brain work?

Your brain takes in information from your body and sorts through it. Then it sends out messages, telling your body what to do.

The messages from your brain are sent along pathways, called **nerves**, that go to every part of your body.

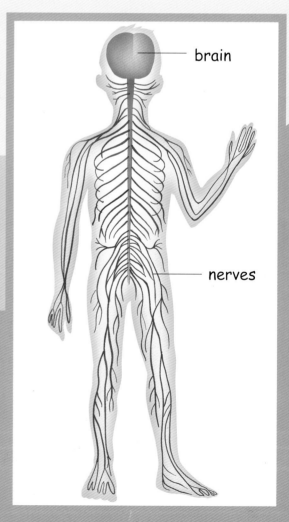

brain

nerves

Your body also sends messages back to your brain about all the things that you do, from seeing and smelling, to moving and eating.

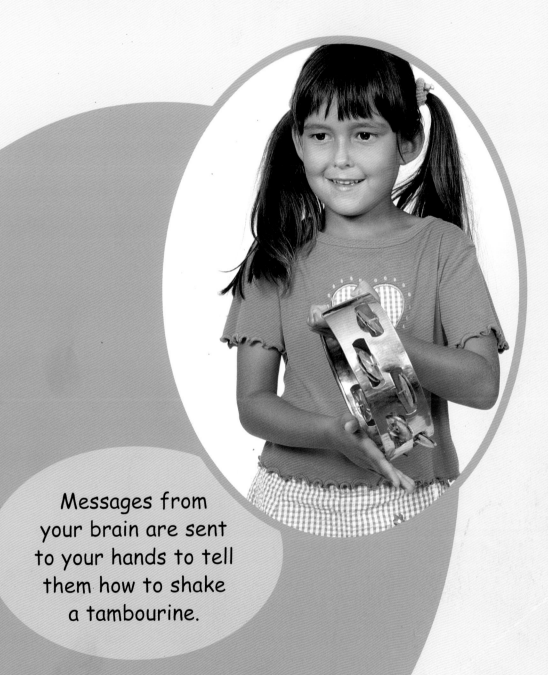

Messages from your brain are sent to your hands to tell them how to shake a tambourine.

Thinking hard

Different parts of your brain do different jobs.
The largest part of your brain is where you think.

The thinking part of your brain helps
you to write a story or a poem.

It lets you speak, understand how to play a video game, solve problems and decide what to do next.

When you look at photographs, your brain helps you think about the happy times you had.

Your brain is made up of two halves. The left half is better at music and art. The right half helps you with sums and science.

Muscle control

The movement area in your brain controls your **muscles**. Muscles are the parts in your body that help you to move.

Your brain sends messages to the muscles in your arms to tell them to catch a ball.

Messages from your brain are sent to your muscles to tell you how to run, jump, skip and hop.

The movement part of your brain helps you to keep your **balance**.

Staying alive

Your brain is in charge of all the things your body must do to keep you alive. It controls how fast your **heart** beats to pump **blood** around your body. It tells your body how to **digest** the food that you eat.

When you eat, messages are sent from your brain to tell your stomach muscles how to squeeze and mash the food.

Your brain does these jobs without you having to think about them.

Your brain tells your **lungs** how to take in air and breathe it out again.

The senses

You have five **senses**. They are sight, hearing, taste, touch and smell.

There are tiny bumps on your tongue called taste buds. They send messages to your brain about the food you eat. Is this sweet or sour, salty or bitter?

Your body sends messages to your brain about all the things you see, hear, smell, touch and taste.

Your skin tells you what things feel like. Pebbles feel hard and smooth.

Learning and memory

When you were a baby, you couldn't do very much. You couldn't walk or talk. But as you grow up, you begin to learn new skills.

A baby's first steps are stored in her memory. Every time she tries to walk, she will go a little further.

Your brain saves information about things you have seen, done and learned in its memory.

Learning to ride a bike is hard, but if you practise, you will soon be able to do it without thinking.

Feeling happy, feeling sad

Do you feel sad if it is raining and you can't go out to play? Do scary stories make you want to run away and hide?

Happiness is a feeling that comes from your brain.

Your brain allows you to feel angry if your little sister has broken one of your toys.

All feelings come from your brain.
It controls every **emotion** you have.

23

Asleep and dreaming

Your brain is always working. Even when you are asleep, it is busy sorting through all the things you have done during the day.

Scientists think that we dream when the brain is sorting through our memories.

Sleep is controlled by different parts of your brain. One part sends you to sleep, while another part wakes you up.

Sleep is very important.
It gives your body a chance to rest.

You sleep for about 26 years during your lifetime.

Looking after your brain

Your brain works very hard for you, so you should look after it.

Your brain is very **delicate**. When you're out roller skating or on a bike ride, wear a helmet to protect your head.

A healthy diet with three meals a day, lots of exercise and plenty of sleep will help to keep your brain working well.

Exercise is good for every part of your body, including your brain. It makes you feel good and keeps you fit and healthy.

Memory game

Ask your friends to play the memory game to see who has the best memory. Gather together ten different things and put them on a tray.

Ask a friend to look at the objects for one minute.

Cover the objects and ask your friend
to try to remember what was on the tray.
To make the game harder, try taking away
some of the objects. Now ask your friend
to tell you which objects are missing.

ability To be able to do something.

balance To be steady and not fall over.

blood The red liquid full of oxygen that is pumped around your body by your heart.

brain The soft part inside your head that controls everything you think and do.

control To be in charge of things that happen.

delicate Something that is very precious and needs to be looked after carefully.

digest To break down food inside the stomach so that it can be used by your body.

emotion The way you feel. Happiness, sadness, anger and fear are all emotions.

heart The muscle that pumps blood around your body.

lungs The soft spongy parts inside your chest that allow you to breathe.

memory The part of your brain that stores information. A memory is also an event from the past that your brain has remembered.

muscles The soft, stretchy parts inside your body that make you move.

nerves The pathways inside your body that carry messages from your brain to all the different parts of the body.

practise To do something over and over again in order to get better at it.

protect To look after someone or something.

senses There are five senses: sight, hearing, taste, touch and smell. They give you information about the world around you.

skull The hard bones inside your head that protect your brain.

Index

ability 4, 30

appearance of brain 6-7

balance 15, 30

blood 16, 30

breathing 17

control 4, 6, 30

digestion 16, 30

dreaming 24

emotions 22-23, 30

exercise 27

feelings 22-23

halves of brain 13

heart 16, 30

learning 20-21

lungs 17, 30

memory 8, 20-21, 28-29, 31

messages 10-11, 14-15, 16

muscles 14-15, 31

nerves 10, 31

practising 21, 31

protection 26-27, 31

senses 18-19, 31

skull 7, 31

sleep 24-25

taste buds 18

thinking 8, 12-13

understanding 13

weight 7